Decodable
READER

UNIT 4

SAVVAS
LEARNING COMPANY

ISBN-13: 978-0-32-898866-2
ISBN-10:   0-32-898866-9

6 21

Table of Contents

A Part of the Past

Written by Andrew Cortes

r-Controlled Vowel *ar*

barn	cart	farm	part

High-Frequency Words

always	new	thank
found	now	think
from	one	
little	please	

We found this in the barn.
We think it is from an old cart.

We found this cart part by the tree.

We ask Gram to please think back.

Gram rode in a cart on the farm
when she was little.

Gram always put the cart back
in the barn.
That was one of her chores.

They got a new farm cart when
my dad was little.

We thank Gram for her help.
We now have a part of the past!

Corn Cakes

Written by Melissa Jarowski

Decodable Book Reader

38

_r_-Controlled Vowel _ar_

card dark hard Mark start

Ending -_es_

finishes mixes

Plural -_es_

batches boxes

High-Frequency Words

always	new	thank
find	please	together
found	said	

Dad makes two batches of corn
cakes for us.
They are not too hot to eat.

10

"Can we make more for Mom,
please?" we ask.

"You can make one new batch
with me," Dad said.
We always like to do things together.

We look at the card.

We use the boxes and milk to start the cakes.
Mark mixes the corn with the rest.

Mark and I find the dark pan.
We are glad we found it!
It always makes good cakes.

Dad finishes the corn cakes.
That was not hard.
"Thank you!" said Mom.

They Work Hard

Decodable Reader 39

Written by Sunil Patel

r-Controlled *er*

clerk	her

r-Controlled *ir*

birds	girl

r-Controlled *ur*

hurt	nurse

High-Frequency Words

any	every	very	works
down	pull	were	

My mom is a clerk in a store.
We were at her store one time.

Her job is to help any kids who
like sports.

She needs to pull down boxes to help this girl.
She will get her the best fit.

If any kids run or jog, my mom
can help.
She works very hard.

My dad is a nurse.
He works with a vet to help birds,
dogs, and cats.

Dad helps every pet that is hurt
or sick.
We were there to see him work
one time.

He works very hard.

A New Shirt

Written by Malika Jones

r-Controlled *er, ir, ur*

clerk	perfect	shirts
first	purse	turn
Herb	shirt	

Adding Endings

digging	matching	started
grabbed	needed	stopping
matched	slipped	zipped

High-Frequency Words

any	every	new	out	said	were
could	found	now	pull	very	would

25

Herb needed a new shirt to match.
They were his best pants.

Mom said to look at every shirt first.
Herb could not see any shirts that
matched his pants.

Mom grabbed her purse.
They zipped to the store.

Herb slipped on any shirt that
they found.
Mom started to pull out more shirts.

The clerk said matching would be
very hard.
Herb said they were not stopping.

It was his turn to look on the shelf.
Herb saw it as he was digging in
a pile of shirts.

Herb felt very glad.
He now has the perfect match!

Yard Sale

Written by Tony Ramos

Comparative Endings

fastest	smaller	taller
shorter	smallest	

High-Frequency Words

away	now	there
light	our	was
never	pretty	

We set up our yard sale.

We will sell our things that do not fit.
We will sell our things that we
never use.

We set up in the yard.
There is a lot of light from the sun.

That pretty blue skirt is a smaller size
than I am now.
Meg is the smallest girl on our block.

This shirt fit when I was shorter.
That ball can go with it.

I am taller now.
It is time to send it away.

That was our fastest sale!

Where Is My Badge?

Written by Erik Perez

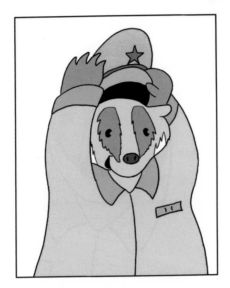

Consonant Pattern *-dge*

badge	ledge
edge	Madge

Word Family *-ink*

pink	wink
think	

High-Frequency Words

a	I	said	the	where
find	of	see	to	your

41

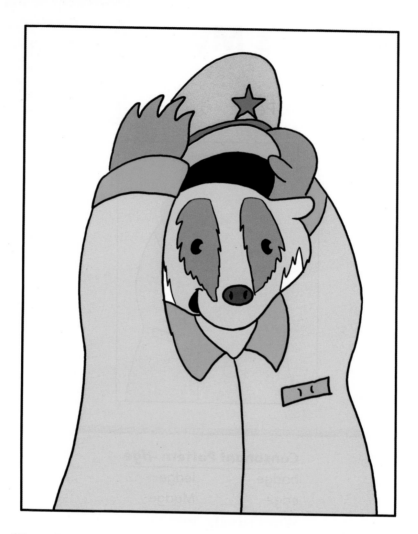

"Let's get my red badge first.
Then I can go,"
Bucky said to Madge.

"Where is my red badge?"
asked Bucky.
"I think I left it on that ledge."

"Is your badge on the edge
of that desk?" Madge asked.
"Did it fall in this trash can?"

"No," said Bucky.
He seemed sadder.
"We can't find my badge."

Madge sat on her bed.
Then she jumped up.
"I see it!" she yelled.

"It is by my pink brush," Madge said.
"Bucky, keep this badge safe.
It is your best badge."

"Thanks, Madge,"
Bucky said with a wink.
He felt glad.

A Storm Tent

Written by John Weston

Diphthong *ow*

down   howl

Diphthong *ou*

clouds   loud   out   sounds

High-Frequency Words

again   lights   soon
both   read

49

The clouds got darker.
It was going to storm soon.

There was a loud bang!
The lights in the house went out.

It was very dark.
The loud sounds came again.
The storm started to howl.

Soon Mom and I got a big sheet.
We made a storm tent.

We sat in the tent in the hall.
How fun!

The lights came back on.
We both sat down in the tent again
to read.

Let's do this for every storm!

On a Farm

Written by Jason Rivera

Diphthong *ow*

cows   down   plow

Diphthong *ou*

flour   ground   hours   proud

Vowel Digraph *ai*

grain   pails

Vowel Digraph *ay*

day   gray   hay   Ray

High-Frequency Words

again   comes   goes   know   soon
both   every   how   read   together

57

Ray and Midge have a big gray barn
for cows.
They have pails of milk for sale
every week.

They both feed hay to the cows.
They both milk the cows every day.

They milk the cows when the sun comes up.
They milk the cows again when the sun goes down.

Ray and Midge plow the ground.

It takes many hours to plant
the crops.

They both read to know more.
Soon they can make flour with grain.

They both know how to do a lot.
They are proud that they do it
together.

Plum Jam

Written by Grace Yoon

Diphthong *oi*
boil   moist

Diphthong *oy*
boy   enjoy

High-Frequency Words

been	does	words
carry	going	

We are going to make some
plum jam.
You can see how we do it.

We look at the words on the card.
We go step by step.

First, we carry the plums to the sink
and wash them.
That does it!

We cut each moist plum.

We boil them with a gift from the bees.

Now the jam needs to rest.
It has been a long day.

Boy, it is good!
Now we can enjoy the plum jam
for weeks!

Small Roy

Written by Trisha Howard

Diphthong *oi*			**Vowel Digraph *ea***	
coin	foil	join	bread	meal
Diphthong *oy*			dream	pea
boy	joy	Roy	leaf	sea
			leaps	

High-Frequency Words

been	could	going
carry	does	word

In his dream, Roy got smaller and
smaller and smaller.
A boy could carry Roy in a pocket.

Roy leaps from leaf to leaf.

Roy could sit on a coin.
He could make a meal of a pea and
a crust of bread.

A bug could join him in a foil raft
going out to sea.

Roy hopes the big dog does not
spot him.

He makes a word in the soil.

It is a joy when Roy wakes up.
It had been a dream!

A Day at the Park

Written by Anita Flores

Adding Endings (Change *y* to *i*)

cried   dried   tried

Long *e:* Vowel Digraph *ea*

dream   Jean   leaf   neat   team   treat

Short *e:* Vowel Digraph *ea*

instead   wealth   weather

High-Frequency Words

a	look	they	was
again	of	three	yellow
are	said	to	
enjoy	the		

Jean and Tom went to this park.
The weather was nice.
At the gate it said,
"Keep this park neat."

"We will treat it well
so that we can enjoy it again,"
Tom said.

"Look at this wealth of trees!"
Jean cried.
"These reds and yellows are
a nice treat."

Tom asked Jean,
"Can we play with that team?"
They played three games.

Then Tom sketched the sky on his
art pad.
Jean tried to sketch a dried leaf
instead.
She made it look nice.

At the lake, Jean and Tom
got to feed the ducks
and see big fish.

At last this fun day ended.
"Such a nice day!" Jean cried.
"It seemed like a dream."

A Fine Fit

Written by Luis Ibarra

Adding Endings

liked	smaller	thinnest
pets	smallest	tried
petting	thinner	wished

Vowel Digraph *ie*

brief	field

High-Frequency Words

give	may	other	said
have	number	right	was

Max had a number of pets in
his shop.
He tried to match the right pet for
each kid.

Beth liked smaller pets.
Max tried a field mouse.

"May I try a smaller pet, please?"
said Beth.
She wished it were thinner like
her tie.

She gave a snake a brief try.

"May I try petting some other small, thin pet, please?"

"Give this bug a try," said Max.
"It is the smallest and thinnest
I have."

She tried it.
It was a fine fit.